Women's Guide to Understanding Men on the Down Low

Women's Guide to Understanding Men on the Down Low

Everything You Need to Know About Straight Men Who Have Sex With Men

Busta

To order additional copies of this book, contact:
Xlibris Corporation
1-888-795-4274
www.Xlibris.com
Orders@Xlibris.com
62716

CONTENTS

Dedicated to both you and myself as well. May this guide bring you peace, awareness, and knowledge to your life. I pray that we accept one another's sexuality and that we be honest with our partner(s). This is my mission to you and the world. A burning desire consumed me. I have been given the secret gift of seeing bisexuality and homosexuality for what it really is. Throughout history, there have been bisexual and homosexual men who have paved the way for the next generation of same-gender-loving men. I began tracing bisexuality and its culture and history. I decided to write this guide to help break the silence, to bring understanding to others. I was amazed at how many men (of all races) secretly have sex with other men while having sex with females or having a girlfriend, fiancée, or wife. Inquisitively, I asked, "Why doesn't everybody know this? Why the secret?" So I began searching for masculine bisexual men of this day and time who have children, are married, or are sexually involved with both males and females. Throughout my investigation, they began to emerge. One bisexual man would link me to another in a perfect chain. Now that I have gathered all the information, I can now bring you *The Women's Guide to Understanding Men on the Down Low.*

We need to stop shying away and ignoring that bisexual men exist. They are reaching out through the expression of sagging their pants in public to make a statement to make their presence known and visible. Our men want to feel at home, safe, and have the opportunity to be open about their sexuality. They want you to be pro-bisexual and to let them know that it's okay to be who they are.

Everyone seems to focus on the bad and negative conflicting views about one's sexuality.

> *How much sense does it make for us to give the problem all of the energy, as oppose to focusing of love, trust, living in abundance, education, employment and peace. (Lisa Nichols)*

ACKNOWLEDGMENTS

Thanks to all who have paved the way for bisexual and gay men in Missouri and Illinois. You will always be remembered. I will immortalize us here in this book. To my brothers who are living this secret, you are loved beyond measure. You may treat your male lover like chopped liver, but have a heart and believe that your male lover loves you just as equally or even more than your wife or girlfriend loves you. Please be fair to your male lover.

Thanks to all bisexual black men for generously and unselfishly sharing your input and insight for this book. You've shown me your tenacity for change.

To my brother who has served time or is currently serving time in the Missouri prison system, thanks for helping me by answering my questions and sharing your stories for the guide.

THE INTRODUCTION

June 2009 Revisited

In no way is this book demonizing or degrading bisexuality in men. It is saying come out and celebrate who you are. You do not need to play games with female's lives, time, and emotions while you have a male lover who is invisible to her and your family. Be fair and play safe.

I do not know if I will be incarcerated or not by the time of the release of this book. Whatever the decision of the judge and jury, I wish to be contacted by all media outlets to get the word out about his matter. So no matter what the result, I want you all to contact me.

Now is the time to rise up as same-gender-loving men and take responsibility for our own personal actions. We are the future for the next generation. We are living in the days of the dreams and the prayers of the slaves. We are living in the time of the first African American president Barack Obama. This is our day and our time to rise above fear, bigotry, prejudice, shame, and denial. Your sexuality is accepted by Jesus Christ. We are all God's children.

Religion has demonized bisexuality and homosexuality, which has made it harder for bisexual and homosexual males to be open and honest. This type of teaching has resulted to men living a lie; being undercover; having feelings of guilt, shame, and denial; and fighting or suppressing their own bisexual nature as if they are doing something that is not right or against God's will.

Bisexual men were also brought to this country as slaves. They also went through struggles. There are so many untold stories of bisexual and homosexual Africans who were brought to the United States as slaves. They have also been raped and molested. We are living in a new day and time. We are living the dream of our ancestors.

Now you can live in freedom and represent for those who have not had this opportunity in this day and time. In their prayers, honor, and memory, represent for them in our time. We need to also find a new movement other than sagging pants. Your message is being seen and recognized; now we must begin a new movement. We must now start pulling up our pants so that we may go further.

Just like the freedom from slavery or the civil rights movement, now is the time for the sexuality freedom movement, of acceptance of bisexual and gay men of color. We cannot continue to be silent. Silence will lead to the death of our bisexual brothers. We must not lose our fathers, sons, uncles, brothers, and cousins to HIV/AIDS, gangs, prison, or running away from home due to them suppressing their sexuality. Sexuality also plays a role in men's behavior and the decisions they make.

Once we face bisexuality, it can also help our men to let them know they are accepted and loved more than they know. Let's save our men from running from their sexuality. Our effort today will save lives tomorrow.

The second moral of this guidebook is for everyone not to get so caught up in the pleasure of the sexual moment, where you allow the desires of your flesh override your common sense of what you know about sexually transmitted diseases and your own personal responsibilities when having sex.

We must take responsibility for our own personal actions when engaging in sex by not putting blame on our sex partner or selfishly thinking of protecting ourselves by accepting and assuming all the risk that come with sexual activity.

Women, stop blaming homosexuals.

Homosexuals, stop blaming women.

Women, stop blaming bisexual men.

Take on your own personal responsibilities for your own behaviors. We are sexual beings; we must begin to accept the fact that bisexual men exist too. Bisexual males have rights also. HIV/AIDS has opened the closet to bisexuality in men. Now is the time to come together and respect one another's sexuality.

Women, do not put blame on your bisexual or gay men. They have been demoralized, degraded, and stereotyped enough by society and the media. Because whenever we see or hear about bisexuality or homosexuality, it is always someone who is looked upon as a negative, feminine, or something to laugh at or to make a mockery of.

We must overcome these stereotypical images and negative emotions as well as opinions and ignorance of what bisexuality and homosexuality looks and/or sounds like.

The purpose of this book is to educate and uplift a society that is in distress through intervention techniques. We can combat negative images and issues regarding the bisexual and homosexual inner-city, urban, ghetto, and hood communities.

Our bisexual brothers deserve the right to be who they are. We must not demonize our men. Isn't it hard enough already for our brothers who are not only dealing with family but also with financial issues? Being prejudged as being undereducated, thugs, beggars, thieves, crooks, robbers, someone who is just up to a con or who is up to no good.

It's a real good tool in terms of bringing the Heterosexual, Bisexual, and Homosexual communities together.

I think we all should understand that those issues that we all face as human beings are issues we have to face together, not separately.

Another purpose of this book is combating bisexuality and homophobia through visibility. While bisexuality and homophobia, in association with HIV/AIDS, remain a problem for the entire community, the impact within the community is magnified, in part, due to fears of rejection, prejudice, and lack of knowledge.

There are some real deep ramifications within our own community in terms of coming out or in terms of identifying oneself as Bisexual or

Homosexual. Some of those ramifications can result in ostracism not only from one's individual place of employment and family but from the community as a whole.

Bisexuality and Homophobia in the poor and working poor communities is definitely an issue that is problematic. Visibility in itself for bisexual and homosexual males in the community is an issue. Unfortunately, religion has been used as a tool to make that even more problematic, which is really sad—it's a beautiful, healing entity, and it's been used in a negative way.

Many men who are bisexual often use religion as a way to speak against homosexuality as a cover-up for their own bisexuality but secretly have sex with other men. Bisexual and homosexual men have been exploited, degraded, and not celebrated. I say to these brothers who are in the church, "God loves you too. It's okay."

One of the most powerful things a person can do even if they are not an activist is be visible.

That's extremely powerful to non-queer people and to queer people who are in the process of coming out. It's an extremely powerful statement that you can give.

In addition to the individual impact that bisexuality and homophobia has on a person's quality of life, it has had a broader impact within the African American community on a variety of levels, from a lack of visible bisexual male role models to the way the community has dealt with HIV/AIDS.

After 30 years we're still seeing a significant impact in terms of new infections within the poor, working poor, inner city and urban communities. A lot of it has to do with the lack of communication, education as well as the fears not being accepted or harmed for being bisexual or gay, especially for men.

The "down low" phenomenon of married men having sex with other men on the sneak, and while not unique to African American men, has become the subject of much debate in particular in the African American community—an undercounted and underserved population which is still emerging from the shadows.

> Guys on the DL are driven by homophobia because they wouldn't dare identify themselves as gay because of the stigma associated with it, and it's even worse because then you have folks in the media saying that the rise of infection among African American women is a result of black men on the DL. So then they're demonizing black men again . . . so now it makes it even harder for someone to actually come to terms with who they are and celebrate it.

> I think that it has made a difference because I think the Midwest is challenging to live in if you are bisexual or gay. And when you're of color, of ethnic background, it can make it even more challenging. So the presence of an entity that addresses those needs in simple visibility, I think it's a great impact.

> I just hope that everyone comes to terms. [To] enjoy themselves, learn their culture and that as an entire community regardless of sexual orientation or sexual lifestyle. We have to always remember that all of it is our culture and we need to celebrate it all, regardless of our ethnic background.

No more wasting time!

Bust your DL man!

The new you begins now!

Many down-low books are written and sugarcoated by black men with college degrees, who are living lavish lifestyles, who cannot tell you anything about the raw urban street version of men on the down low as I can. This book will save your overall health, life, and family as you know it.

This should have been the first original tell-all book about the down low. Here is the ghetto, urban, inner-street version of the down low from the infamous Busta. This book is where the down-low secret society and alliance will be completely exposed. This will allow women to have a choice to decide. There were so many reasons why I decided to write this book. It has come to this! I am a totally gay man who has had sex with men who claim to be straight.

DL men tell their gay partner(s) all about their girls or wives.

I felt the need to reveal the secrets of men on the down low, who are cowards by misleading women. You will get the secrets, warning signs, and tips. You will receive the answers to the most common questions females ask and must know.

We, as gay men, get used and mistreated by these so-called straight men. These so-called straight men use gay males just for sex, sex in exchange for money and/ or a place to stay. These bisexual men who have private secret sex with gay males wine and dine their girl or wife, while their homosexual lover is used just for sex and is invisible to DL men's girlfriends, wives, families, and friends. Well, until now because I am calling them out. Women have a right to know. I will tell it all. There is more in book 2. Book 1 is just to get the word out, and book 2 will not be a book to play with. Meaning it will be harsh, direct, and in-your-face. I need to take some writing courses and learn what I can and cannot say or use in my book. (This is book 1, where I am playing it safe.)

Once I learn what I can and can't say in a book without being sued or have any other legal issues, once you receive book 2, you will be fully armed to defend yourself against the DL men in your life. I will use people, places, locations, names, and drop all the details.

Book 2 will be off the chain. I expect to have lots of and television interviews where my identity will be withheld until book 2 is released.) You may ask why I need to hide. Because this book is a very seriously dangerous tell-all book, which DL men do not want to come out and who may resort to all means necessary to stop book 2 from being released. I am telling everything about the secret society of bisexuality among masculine men. I must make sure females are fully equipped with all details and information required. No one can tell you if their man is on the down low like a punk, bitch ass, faggot from the urban, inner-city, ghetto, and hood projects as I can.

There are many people in St. Louis, Missouri; Chicago, Illinois; and Atlanta, Georgia; who played a major role in helping me bring this book to you. I have interviewed and surveyed hundreds of everyday bisexual (DL) men who are urban, working poor, or inner-city who identify themselves as straight and have sex with other men, where the female companion is totally unaware of this type of behavior.

Just to get the word out, I am starting off with book 1. This reveals most secrets. Once I take a few writing courses to learn the basics of writing, I will bring you book 2, which will be more professionally revised, more descriptive in detail, and more structured.

Also, I have done an HIV/AIDS investigation and discovered some disturbing information that everyone must be aware of. One out of three African American men has HIV/AIDS. One out of three do not even know they have it, while one out of three are HIV-negative.

You never hear about HIV/AIDS in the media until a well-known person comes out of the closet about having the virus. When we hear HIV/AIDS today, it seems like everyone wants to start asking who has it instead of asking how to show support.

As a woman, you have every right to know if your man is having sex with other men. His deception is the main reason women in urban inner cities are getting infected with the incurable HIV/AIDS. We must save our women. Without females, we cannot reproduce and we will fall as a species. Our efforts through this book today will save lives tomorrow.

Unlike other down-low books, I am giving you the raw urban street version. This book is just my freshman book. I am an amateur writer from the poor streets of the ghetto and hood. Now is the time to hear the story from the perspective of someone from the streets.

PART ONE

The Secrets Revealed

CHAPTER 1

The Secrets Revealed

At a young age, men are taught that boys should be with girls and girls should be with boys. Homosexuality and bisexuality has always been a taboo topic that gets shunned and not to be spoken of. Religion has contributed to most of young men's beliefs that bisexuality and homosexuality is an abomination to God and that homosexuals go to hell. Religion and sexuality has always been in a debate.

One thing that pisses the hell out of me is when I hear women say they are losing their men to other men or when they say, "All that dick is just going to waste." This is what I have to say to those of you who feel this way: "You have so many options and a variety of men to choose from. Do you mean to tell me you cannot find a straight man?"

Our bisexual and homosexual males have struggled being accepted for many years for their sexuality. Many poor, inner-city, urban bisexual and homosexual males have gone as far as running away or leaving home at an early age, giving themselves over to the street life, joining gangs, just being around others who share their bisexual issues. The choices they make maybe negative or violent which may lead them to prison. On that thought, many of our bisexual and homosexual brothers who are serving time in prison tell me that they run the prisons and the lifestyle is more accepted behind bars than in the streets. They took the trend of sagging off their pants in prisons to sagging them in public. The message is to be seen and identified and to represent their bisexuality or homosexuality through dress (sagging pants).

HIV AND AIDS has exposed bisexuality in men and has opened the closet of what being gay looks like and the way feminine homosexual men carry themselves; the same goes for masculine bisexual and gay as well. Many homosexual traits and codes signals allow fellow homosexuals to know they are also homosexuals. HIV/AIDS was known as the gay disease, which meant if you are a feminine gay man, you automatically was accused of or assumed to have HIV/AIDS. Gay men took their dress codes, signals, and traits as well as their mannerisms to appear more masculine and pass themselves off as straight because they do not want to be associated with the stigma, which was "if you are gay, you carry HIV/AIDS". Their gay codes/traits have been stolen and taken over by a secret society of bisexual men. Not only this, the bisexual men made the gay trends/codes their own and took it to a new level of extreme. This is a very smooth, silent trend that has evolved into the mainstream. Bisexual and gay men protest against the homophobic stigma and stereotypes through dress.

Nowadays, it may be kind of difficult to distinguish straight, bisexual, and gay men from one another. Well, this is the part where I will first break it down, explain it.

Hooped earrings: Worn small on one or both ears is the code men use to signal other men. These hooped rings mean one is bisexual.

Sagging pants/jeans: We already know gay prisoners use this code to signal other men that they have sex with men. One who sags his pants is a form of nonverbal communication that means he is bisexual gay or the one who wants to get penetrated. This is a trend that has evolved from the prisons to the streets, which carries the same meaning but with more power. They are sagging in honor, memory, and respect of their fellow bisexual brothers who may never see the streets again and as well as a commemoration. Bisexual men use this code today. If you ask them "Why do you wear your pants like that? Why do you sag your pants?" they will reply, "It's just what we do," which when translated is saying, "We are combating bisexuality and homophobia through visibility. We are putting a face on bisexuality and homosexuality. We are being proactive in breaking the silence and stigma of bisexuality and homosexuality through visibility by sagging our pants. It's also a silent protest for equal rights among the dominant heterosexuals. No straight heterosexual man should be sagging his pants. This code or trend is for bisexual and gay men. Period!"

Money and drugs: Along with the sagging of the pants/jeans, it does not mean he sells drugs, but he just might do that as well. It is also a code that he will have sex with another male in exchange for cash, drugs, or lodging.

Trade is the commonly used term by gay men, which usually means men who look straight and whom you cannot tell if they had sex with other men just by looking at them. It also may define sexual roles they play in bed during sexual activity. *Trade* also means sex with another male in exchange for cash, drugs, or lodging.

Here is the breakdown. Bisexual men will argue with these true facts. Openly gay men use this to signal to other gay men. This was stolen by bisexual men. In bisexual men's defense, they still remain hiding behind the straight label while using gay trends and codes. They still will deny these codes that mean they have sex with other men. They have stolen these gay signals, codes, and traits, called them their own, and gave them a masked meaning.

Men who have sex with men who identify themselves as straight (heterosexual) feel as if they are not gay or bisexual because of the stigma that is attached to the words *bisexual* or *gay*. There are several types of men who have sex with men who identify themselves as straight.

These are the masculine men you'd never suspect. It is a myth that bisexual and gay men are feminine, slim, and pretty faced. Bisexual and homosexual men come in all shapes and sizes.

In most major urban areas such as St. Louis, Missouri; Chicago, Illinois; and Atlanta, Georgia; men who do not receive penetration in their rectums feel that they are not the ones who are gay because they are not the ones who are receiving penetration. In the gay community, these men are called tops. These top men who have sex with men label themselves as straight (heterosexual) because they don't receive penetration. This is common. Please read "Answers to the Most Common Questions Women Ask about the Down Low."

This is just book 1 of 2. In book 2, I am really gonna be even more raw, direct, and uncut. So look for it once I reach my two thousand plus copies sold from this book. So let me know you want more by supporting book 1. I promise to give you a comprehensive book 2.

CHAPTER 2

Answers To The Most Common Questions Women Ask About The Down Low

M y man is not on the down low!
Think again.

Q. How can I tell if my man is on the down low?
A. Who are his friends? Do you know them all? You should know your man's friends and be suspicious of his new friend or a friend of his that you never have seen. Or if he plays in your clothes.

Straight men that are secure with their sexuality will not be homophobic. Your man is on the DL if you ask him if he is bisexual and he gets very pissed off, angry, upset, or may even be violent toward you or homosexuals due to his own insecurities of his sexuality or lifestyle.

Q. Where do DL men go to meet other DL men?
A. The picking up or meeting of DL men is by networking through gay males, hanging out in the streets, bus/train station stops, straight clubs, and bars. (This is where many DL men congregate.) The DL men visit their gay male friend's home from time to time. This is where the DL men go to hopefully run into other DL men from the neighborhood. The gay man knows who most other neighborhood DL men are. This is one of the options DL men use to meet other DL and gay men.

When DL men meet other DL men, they tend to form their own small private social network among others who share a similar interest.

Q. How do DL men know if another man is on the DL? How do they notice one another?

A. Other than going to the gay man's home to meet other DL men, they also meet other DL men on their own. They say eye contact. But there is more than just eye contact. DL men notice one another first based on eye contact, then facial expression, next conversation. Let me explain. Two DL men or a gay man and a DL man will always demand mutual eye contact through nonverbal communication. Facial expressions are then established within seconds to confirm if they are approachable or defensive. If both the eye contact and facial expression are confirmed to be positive, then they start an icebreaker conversation. Their first initial conversation is usually about the game or a hobby. Men who are not mutually interested or attracted toward one another cut the conversation short.

A. Another form of nonverbal communication among men who have sex with men is the sagging of their pants. They use this form of nonverbal communication to signal a potential mate, friend, or partner. The old trend of wearing long T-shirts, which they called tall tees, have been played out. Wearing tall tees meant the male received penetration.

Q. What if I suspect my man is on the down low?

A. Investigate! Then decide on your own what decisions you should make.

Q. Why DL men just cannot be honest about being bisexual/gay?

A. The bisexual (DL) man are very smart and protective and want to be accepted into society. They feel like they will be embarrassed or seen as less masculine. They have seen the example of abuse, stigma, harassment, prejudices, bigotry, and sexism their fellow gay counterparts have struggled with. These experiences have pushed them further back into the closet. But HIV/AIDS is forcing them out of the closet to find themselves having to reveal themselves to females, family, and society.

Still, to this day, gay men are paving the way for bisexual (DL) men. But still, DL males stray from their male lovers to hide behind a female to protect his heterosexual image/label. The DL men wants to feel accepted and be a part of a family and will not risk being labeled as gay, which in his mind means less of a man, weak, or feminine. Most DL men are totally masculine with no indication of being weak, soft, fem, or any homosexual stereotypes.

Bisexual DL men find it more acceptable to be seen with a female in public and around family than being with his male sex partner or male companion.

Q. Are DL men the reason many women contract HIV/AIDS?
A. Yes! HIV is contracted mainly from someone who receives penetration or someone who gives head. At some point, the HIV-positive man contracted the virus from either getting penetrated or giving head through unprotected sex with an infected male. Most straight men contract HIV from intravenous drug use or unprotected sex with an infected female drug user or sex worker. It is very difficult for a female to get infected with the virus. Two HIV-negative men cannot give each other HIV. You can only get HIV from unprotected sex with an infected person.

CHAPTER 3

What Women Need To Know

Females are smarter than men. Use your instinct. If you suspect it, chances are you're right. I can give you a list of red flags. First off, women, please find another new age way to figure out if a man is straight or not. Stop using these questions to try to figure out if your man is on the down low or gay: Do you have any children? Do you have a girlfriend? Are you married? Even if he says yes to any of these questions, it does not mean he is straight.

Bisexual men want to marry women and have kids too. They feel they have the right to reproduce, have a family, and to keep a part of themselves here after they pass away.

Many bisexual men who have sex with men will deny any type of sex with another guy. Even if you catch them in the act, they may still give you every excuse in the book to why they did it.

He has this mystery male friend you may have never seen, never met, or never known existed. But he always seem to go by this guy's house often or either on the first or second week of the month. You may or may not know this guy your man goes to see, but the other guy knows all about you. Read more on this in chapter 8, "Your Man's Lover Knows You, but You Don't Know Him."

Your man just may be bold enough to introduce you to his male lover but will address him as his friend, buddy, or partner. Red alert! The male sex partner may have a girlfriend or wife also. Remember, chances are he is not going to introduce you to some obviously gay dude. The guy he introduces to you may be just as handsome and masculine as your man. This is done to throw you off their trail. Also it helps with your man's reputation to pass himself off as straight, not only to both your family and his, but also for the community and society to view him as straight (heterosexual).

Your man's secret male sex partner may also be a transsexual or cross-dresser. In today's time, men want men who look like females due to society's view on homosexuality and their own insecurities.

Your DL man and his male companion both know your schedule, routine, when to call one another, and when and how to cheat on you.

Your man may also be bold enough to have sex with his male sex partner in your bed.

There are codes that men who have sex with other men use. These codes are mentioned in "The Secrets Revealed" (chapter 1).

It only takes as little as fifteen minutes for them to have an encounter and then go their separate ways.

A faithful family man does not need friends. All he needs is his family and job. If he always has to hang with his boy more than you, take this as a red flag.

DL men do not want obviously gay men to speak or acknowledge them in public or around others. DL men get very nervous when a homosexual is around because chances are the homosexual knows of his secret lifestyle.

Just because your man lays it down correctly in bed and gives it to you often, it does not men he is straight. It just might mean he likes to use his penis. Remember, you are a cover-up. He wants you and the world to see him as a straight heterosexual man.

Women, go to a gay bar. You might see your man there.

Gay males meet gay men at straight clubs/bars (which you will read in the next chapter).

Cell phones and the Internet are the new tool DL men use to social network without you being aware of. You should know every person in his phone directory and have access to his e-mail accounts.

Be suspicious of your man's friends who are too eager to give your man money. Chances are, this guy is either your man's trick or lover.

Your man's best or closest friend may also be your man's lover. Do not let the fact that your man's friend is married or have children fool you.

Metrosexual is just a new term for bisexual or gay. Remember that bisexual men steal gay males' trends and call them their own then flip the script.

Most DL men only have sex with other men when they're visiting another state. This gives them the opportunity to have sex with other men in another city where they are not really known, and this also decreases the chances of their bisexual lifestyle from being exposed.

Masculine men have sex with other masculine men to throw you off their trail.

Bisexual DL men want to appear as the victim when they are the culprit.

Women are naturally smarter than men.

I want to speak to all of you more about this in details in which I know you want to read and hear. I need your help. This is book 1 of book 2. I am testing the waters on this first book to see how everyone receives it. I really need to see how it does in the market. When I see that there is a large demand for a more detailed book, I will bring it to you. I need your support. Once I reach two thousand books sold, I will start on book 2, which is very graphic and of adult content. I have been forbidden, limited, and somewhat silenced from speaking candidly in this book until I learn my rights and the laws. Women, you deserve the right to have a straight heterosexual man who is honest and not an honest liar.

CHAPTER 4

DL Men And Gay Men Meet Up At Straight Clubs/Bars

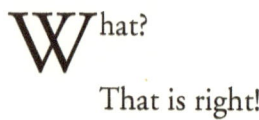hat?

That is right!

The most popular place for DL men and gay men to meet are straight clubs and straight bars. You ask how that is? Or why that is? Due to gay prejudices, labels, and stereotypes, men feel more comfortable going to places that are not labeled or known as gay. For decades, bisexual men and most gay men feel more comfortable and secure at clubs and bars that are labeled straight.

Many bisexual men go to straight clubs to meet females, but their alternative goal is to meet and establish social network with other DL men in the club and bar scene who share common interest. Both gay and bisexual men know this and now so do you. So the next time you're at the club, notice how the men party among one another and not females.

Masculine men who have sex with other men know which straight clubs to attend where they can meet other men like themselves.

Here is the basic rundown. Bisexual men primarily seek females at straight clubs and bars. Gay men primarily seek the bisexual (DL) men. Bisexual (DL) men are basically with females as a cover-up and façade to appear and pass himself off as straight or to catch the interest of another man who shares his DL interest because society has pressured and shamed him, which has caused him to suppress his natural God-given interest, lust, love, and physical bodily contact for another male in public as he would a female.

Gay men are on the sidelines at straight clubs/bars to intercept and conquer the masculine DL man for himself. Usually, the gay male has to wait on the sidelines. If the DL man does not get any play with a female at the club, he resorts to the gay guy. First, the initial eye contact and body language. While this is happening, there are lots of unpleasant tension, hostility, and body language between the bisexual and the gay male that goes unnoticed by the average straight men and straight women in the club/bar.

When a DL man doesn't get any play from a female that night at the club, he discreetly makes his move to the gay male that has been on the sidelines all night. The gay guy already knows he has to play this game. But I am going to also put you up on the game as well.

Here's the play. The DL man did not or may not have gotten the number of sexual hookup from the females for the night. So he needs to get laid. They may have been watching and clocking the men all night. The gay male will see the DL man's disappointment as an opportunity to present himself to the DL man. They do not have sex in the club or expose themselves. I will share with you two things that take place next. The gay or the DL man will offer the other a drink and start a conversation; before the drink is even bought, both guys already know what time it is. The second thing that may happen is that one may either ask the other to meet him in the restroom or follow the other into the restroom. The straight clubs'/bars' restrooms are where they go to exchange numbers or make arrangements for hooking up, and they can talk more openly out of the presence of females. DL men do not worry about other men seeing or hearing them conversing in the restroom.

What to Look for while at the Straight Club/Bar to Assure You Are with a Straight Man and Not a DL, Bisexual Man

> If you notice that the man you are with is distracted, irritated, agitated by another guy in the club/bar, he maybe on the down low. A straight man will not worry or trip off another man's lifestyle, behavior, or sexual orientation.

> DL men and gay men are the main ones in the club who refer to women as girls, bitches, and whores.

Usually DL men go out to straight clubs/bars with his gay man sex partner. Beware! The gay lover is the one who is off to the side with a slight negative attitude toward you, but you may not even think nothing of this or even notice it. When you are talking to a man in the club, his friend(s) should not be too close by. If so, beware.

The gay dude is the straight man's friend. (Yeah right.)

The man you are with goes to the restroom too many times or stays in the restroom too long. If so, it means that he noticed another DL or gay male and followed him to the restroom, and they are in there either trying to see what's up or exchanging numbers.

DLs and gay men nowadays refer to one another as mentor, friend, buddy, or partner.

DL men have a strong desire to be in an environment that makes him feel comfortable and his sexual lifestyle is not being made obvious or on display.

"Many situations have gone down in the club where you may think it's two guys fighting or shooting at the clubs over some female. In most situations like this, they're fighting or shooting because the bisexual or the homosexual felt that he was disrespected by his partner by flirting with a female when they are out at the club together," says a police officer.

CHAPTER 5

Other Down-Low Books

My version is straight from the urban, inner-city, ghetto projects and the streets.

Like I have mentioned before, many DL books are authored by intelligent professionals with college degrees. They are not on my lower level to bring it to you from a street perspective as I do. I know the street version. I am the street version.

One author of one of those DL books speaks about being married and living a secret life with men, which his wife was totally unaware of. (Yeah right!) She may have suspected it, then found out. I could have just looked at his face and told her that she was with a gay man. Why do we have this gay man writing a book about the down low? I could have told her he was gay just by looking at him. He is a poor example of what a DL man looks like. Please give us a more handsome DL man to represent for the DL men. Now she has a book out about how she did not know her man was gay. (Laughing out loud.) Did you know that you have to ask a gay man if your man is a straight man? Do what any smart woman would do. Here's a secret revealed: ask a homosexual if he thinks your man is bisexual (DL). It takes a man to know if another man has sex with men. This is a natural instinct men who have sex with men have. This intuition is real.

The other DL book I have read is also by a Missouri native. Middle class, educated, attractive, I cannot say anything negative about this brother. Much love to him and his successes, achievements in the gay community and HIV/AIDS advocacy.

My audience I wish to reach are the poor, working poor, undereducated, disadvantaged, and the urban inner-city communities who have disproportionately the highest HIV/AIDS infection rate.

Also, this is the only book on the market today from a totally gay man who has had sex with DL men. One female had no idea that I existed in her man's life. She has no idea her man has sex with gay men. Allow me to tell all dirt in my next book. In the meantime, continue to read and enjoy the book, and I promise you that book 2 will be a revised, updated, detailed version so you will be well equipped for the bisexual (DL) men in your life that you are not aware of.

Call me a home wrecker or whatever you like. But what responsibilities does he have? I feel that he is using me just for sex while flaunting you like a trophy. We both are being played with. I am tired of being the secret of his life. I want to be treated with love and affection. I want to be able to go out and be in public with him, just the same as you do. But he wants me to be kept in the shadows until now.

My ex-lover may try to prevent book 2 from being published. Ladies, now is the time to be totally aware of the DL men. I am constantly looking over my shoulder; he may come to retaliate against me for this book release. This is why I will continue to withhold my identity until I get secured protection from my ex-lover. He is a very well-known athlete and financially secure enough to attack me in any manner at any time.

For me to mention his name will cause citywide drama and controversy. He may even try to use his money to make me disappear into the prison system or by death. But I need him to know that my memory and spirit will survive through this book. Even if or when I am gone, the book will always be left in my memory. I will be immortalized via this book. But if anything were to ever happen to me, by my ex-lover or by anyone, I want him to be the first person to be interrogated on this investigation. Also I want you all to know that I am here now in the land of the living and my mission is to do the forbidden. That's to expose the DL society head-on in book 2.

PART TWO

Secrets Revealed—
Down-Low Men Speak

CHAPTER 6

DL Men Answer Your Questions

I have interviewed hundreds of men. Here are the most common answers to my questions.

Q. Why do you *not* tell women you are bisexual (DL)?

I am a selfish, self-centered person. I did not think or feel that it mattered. It's just sex, and sex is natural.

I do not tell because they do not need to know because I am only having situational sex with other males but plan on being with a female long-term. Fucking with males is just something to do when I get horny.

I am not bisexual. I am not gay. I am a straight man. I love women. There is nothing to tell her. I am supposed to be with a female. But I cannot resist my attraction to males whenever the opportunity presents itself.

Q. You're a grown man. Why do you lie?

Everyone wants to be accepted and to fit into society's mold of what is righteous. I was taught to suppress my love and sexual attraction to males. So I hide my true bisexuality by having a female as my girl.

Q. How do you maintain a double life?

Most men told me *time*. They said they have to keep tabs on the time.

They call their male sex partner to arrange a place, time, and date for the sexual encounter (usually at the gay male's place). After the sexual encounter with their male partner(s), the deal is to act and carry on as if the sexual encounter never happened. Yes, denial is very acceptable in the DL lifestyle. They lie to deceive because of the stigma.

Q. What would you do if she found out?

Everyone said if she did not actually see it, they would deny it till the end.

If she actually sees it with her own eyes, I would feel trapped and exposed and would have to submit to her blackmail or extortion in exchange for her silence.

Q. What type of gays do you like? With this question, I received lots of diverse answers.

Most men said they preferred transsexuals, cross-dressing men.

Many DL men said they prefer other masculine DL men who are also married or have girlfriends. This way they both have something in common and have more chemistry in and out of bed. Some men want to meet other men who look just as straight as they are so they can take them around their female and family members without it being obvious that they are lovers.

Q. Are you the giver or the receiver?

Many married men have told me that they penetrate their wives but get penetrated by their male sex partners.

Q. Who knows you're bisexual? They answered as follows:

Only the males I have sex with.

Other dudes who may see me out at the gay bars/clubs.

My kids know, but their mom does not know.

Q. Tell me why you treat females differently from your gay lover? I mean, you flaunt and show off your female to family and friends, but you keep your male lover invisible. The most common answers are as follows:

I am a bit ashamed or embarrassed to be seen with my male sex partner because I am so worried about the opinions and acceptance of family and strangers.

I do not want my male sex partner to slip up and make it obvious to others, so the best thing for me and my male sex partner to do is to just keep it in the closet and talk in secret codes.

I am supposed to be with a female, and it's the right thing to do.

Male-to-male sex is wrong and/or a sin and an abomination to God, but I get weak and backslide.

My family pressures me to be with a female, but my urge is to be with another male. I take advantage of the opportunity to have sex with other males when I have the time, plus, I am straight because I am not the one getting fucked.

I just do it for the money, a place to sleep or stay.

My business is not for her to know. I am just doing something.

I love and care about her and want to spend my life with them.

Females are my cover-up to help me appear and pass myself off as a straight man so I can be accepted and treated like a person and not treated in a certain way based on my sexual orientation.

Not having a female under my arm or not being with a female is a sign of being less of a man. Although I love both men and women, I must present a female to uphold my masculine image; anything else would make me fall into the gay stereotypes, which are fem, soft, funny, or less masculine or less respected as a man.

Q. But you've grown. You live alone and pay your own bills. Why have both a female and a male? Your male partner knows about her, but she does not know about him. Don't you feel that is wrong?

I am bisexual. I love pussy, but I like to get fucked up my ass by another male. Having a female is the thing to do. He can know about her because he can understand and accept me more, but she gets the quality time. It's like an investment in my reputation/image.

My job and family wants me to be with a female. So I feel like I am obligated to please my family and keep my job by living a lifestyle that society is more accepting of.

I would rather die and take my bisexuality to my grave with me rather than have my bisexuality exposed and take a chance at experiencing the taunting gay males have gone through. I want to be seen as a man and treated like a man and not be treated as if I am less of a man just because I have sex with men.

CHAPTER 7

Straight Men
Who Have Sex With Men

What? You ask. I know you're saying, "That does not make any sense." You're saying, "If a man is having sex with another man, that means he is gay or bisexual." The secret society of men who have sex with men is very controversial about being called gay so they feel more comfortable with being identified as straight heterosexual because the term is more acceptable. With regard to the African American culture, the term *gay* means weak, soft, sweet, feminine, or even vulnerable. In the African American community, this is the common stereotype, which makes the masculine men who sleep with men to lean more toward using the term *straight/heterosexual.* Those who are gay are looked upon as a spectacle, a circus clown, or something to laugh at and made a mockery of by the African American community as well. These are some of the many reasons why masculine men who have sex with men hide their true sexual identity.

Masculine men who are sexually attracted to other men have this unofficial secret society or alliance. Here's the breakdown:

Masculine men who seek other masculine men only.

Masculine men who seek cross-dressing men or transsexuals only.

Masculine men who seek fem men that's non-cross-dressing/transsexual.

Fem men who seek other fem men.

Regardless of whether the man is either feminine or masculine, it does not define his sexual role.

Many men find one another attractive and get sexually aroused by one another too, just as well as females. It's just more acceptable for those of the opposite sex to make passes at one another. Men who find other men attractive resort to eye contact and start a conversation, and it is less direct than it would be when he is making a pass at a female.

Masculine men who are attracted to other masculine men first make mutual eye contact followed by an innocent statement or question. These statements or questions lean more toward things like sports, hobbies, or interests, which then leads to if they both like females. Once they find a common interest, they will exchange personal information to keep in touch.

Relationships between male and male go deep, so deep that it's considered a delicacy. DL men believe that their lifestyle must be protected among other same-gender-loving men who are also on the down low.

CHAPTER 8

Your Man's Lover Knows You, But You Do Not Know Him

Thank God, I can vent this topic. Many gay males, including myself, can tell you about all these bisexual men who are not only on the down low but are also lowdown. I have met men who tell me all about their females and their relationships with women but the women have no idea of the men's alternative lifestyle. You would think these DL men were more connected to their male sex partners since the gay male sex partner knows all. But that is not the case.

DL men discuss you to their male sex partners but will not discuss them to you. I will explain why this is so in book 2. For now, let me get back to this chapter.

DL men will tell their male sex partner/lover about any of the following:
Your family situation

Your job/occupation

Your living arrangement

Your relationship status

Your man's male sex partner knows you. (He may even know your face and see you more often than you know.) To you, he is a total stranger or he could be your man's masculine straight-looking friend, leaving you with no clue or idea of their relationship.

I as well as my other gay male friends will also tell you that your man will tell his male sex partner everything about you while leaving you totally unaware of what's going on. It takes a gay man to tell you if your man is really straight or not.

PART THREE

Busta Tells All Dirt

CHAPTER 9

The Urban Inner-City Version Of The Down Low

The poor, working poor, and middle-class version of the down low straight out of the ghetto, streets, and the hood, know what I am talking about. So take this seriously. This book is not fiction. I have interviewed hundreds of men who say they are heterosexual (straight). As you have read in part 2, "Down-low Men Speak," now here is where I break this down so you can really understand.

Bisexual (DL men) are cold-blooded, deceiving guys. Ladies, I am that real black homosexual (fag, punk, and sissy) that's not gonna play or sugarcoat my book. I am giving you raw data from the streets and urban communities. You are armed with the book as a weapon to protect yourself from selfish bisexual men.

I am a total homosexual, not bisexual. The homosexual usually just gets the sex from your man. He tells the homosexual all about you, his family, and his workdays. The homosexual must just shut up and be invisible, nonexistent. Well, sisters, through this book, I am telling all in Missouri and Illinois.

Your man knows when to cheat. It takes a small window of opportunity for him to do it. By the time he brings you home a sexually transmitted disease, it's too late to say, "Where in the hell was I when this shit was going on?" asking yourself, "Why I didn't see the signs?" Be very afraid to have sex with your man after reading this book. Get tested for sexually transmitted diseases as soon as possible. Missouri's inner-city women are carrying HIV/AIDS. Most women do not want to know if they are carrying the virus. Others do not even think they're being cheated on. Wake up! Do not let your guard down.

CHAPTER 10

HIV/AIDS
(We Have Failed Our Youth)

With all the information we know about HIV/AIDS, we have failed our youth.

In my preteenage years, herpes was the sexually transmitted disease everyone in the hood was talking about. I can recall my mother always talking about people dying from pneumonia. I came to find out this pneumonia that people was dying from in the ghetto was now given a name. It was called HIV. HIV came along in the mid-1980s. The human immunodeficiency virus was known as a white gay man's disease. Now we can say that those people who died from pneumonia may have died of HIV/AIDS.

HIV/AIDS was the talk of the community among teens in the 1990s.

In the late 1990s, the incurable HIV/AIDS message did not reach the children who may have been too young to know anything about sex or this virus. The teens and older adults failed to mention this disease to many of the children who are now teenagers or young adults carrying the virus.

It hurts my heart when I meet teens and young adults who are HIV-positive. Many tell me they did not get the message.

We need to put HIV/AIDS back on the radar. Too many of our children, friends, and family members are getting infected. We must take the initiative to help stop the spread of this virus that is destroying our community.

HIV/AIDS is the new crack that is destroying the community. You ask the following:

Why do our youth not want to work?

Why can't our people keep a stable, steady job?

Why did he/she run away or leave home?

Why did you drop out or not continue your education?

Why are you always tired and you haven't done anything?

Why beg, steal, or use drugs?

HIV/AIDS is the new crack. I mean, it is the new disease to keep us down and to keep us from succeeding as a community. I want to really go there with you in this book about HIV/AIDS and the impact it has on the families and the community as a whole. I cannot say much now in this book. I really want to go there! I will put the health department, city, and state on blast in book 2. For now, I must play it safe.

Before you get tested for HIV/AIDS, here are what they won't tell you but want you to do and you should not do:

Do not get tested if you do not already have a life or medical insurance policy.

Always do anonymous testing. Once your name is in the system, your life and medical insurance will rise high.

If you need to know if you are HIV-positive or not, do a home HIV/AIDS test.

This is all I can say about this for now.

Please follow these instructions before you get tested for HIV/AIDS.

CHAPTER 11

DL Men's True Chronicles

Facts From the Poor, Working Poor, and Middle-Class Version of the Down Low

Most masculine men who are attracted to other masculine men are discriminating and prejudiced toward their fellow feminine men; there is internalized shame, embarrassment, hatred, and jealousy among most feminine bisexual/gay males and masculine bisexual/gay males. There are so many different combinations. Just like math. So I will use this section to share with you quotes from both sides. Masculine and so-called straight-looking and straight-appearing bisexual and homosexual males find themselves in competition and nonverbal battles with one another due to various reasons. I will explain in book 2.

Back to the chapter at hand. Many bisexual men have been taught that if he has sex with another male, he should be getting paid for it. Most bisexual men go as far as carrying out this teaching, which we call situational sex.

Situational sex is when a bisexual man may need sexual release and usually a gay male will give it up quicker than a female. Situational sex may be sex in exchange for money for bills or to give to his female or for milk and Pampers for their child.

This same type of male labels himself as straight heterosexual because in his mind, this sexual encounter is not considered as an emotional attachment and it is just sex. Since he is not the one who is receiving penetration in his rectum, he considers himself a straight heterosexual male. Here is another obstacle bisexual men face. They have sex with other men and still say they are straight heterosexual because this is what they have been taught to believe. They are taught to believe that sex with other men is not right and it is against God and are taught that they will not enter the kingdom of heaven. Bisexual men are again taught at an early age to repent and ask for God's forgiveness of the sin and to find a woman.

We have bisexual men in the church! Some are pastors, deacons, and so on.

They too are taught that bisexuality and homosexuality is a sin, an abomination to God. Yet these same men who speak against it have male lovers. See, they will also have sex with other males and speak against bisexuality and homosexuality and they are like that themselves.

I have asked several men in the church, "Why do it then deny it?"

They have all told me that their position in the church and their reputation in the community has a lot to do with it. Also they have told me that they deny and speak against bisexuality and homosexuality because it's what people want to hear. What many do not realize is that this is why our bisexual men get confused and misdirected.

Bisexual and homosexual males need role models, and when the church turns them away, they resort to negative behavior. Within this negative behavior, they find what they have been looking for all along, and that is sanctuary.

The church must stop being hypocrites themselves. God's house is for all people! If poor, urban inner-city bisexual males do not have anything, we must not deny them church. Stop speaking against bisexuality and homosexuality in the church for Jesus Christ is our Lord and Savior too.

"God so loved the world he gave his only begotten son. He whomsoever believes in him shall not perish, but have everlasting life."

The Bible says *whomsoever*!

I am sick and tired of our gay and bisexual men who are totally gay going around saying they are straight and praying to God to send them the right woman. To you, I say, "How does that make your male lover feel when you say that?"

To all of you who are bisexual or homosexual, speak out. By you speaking out about being bisexual, you could help someone better their lives and help them in making better, more positive decisions.

Show these other bisexual and homosexuals that they can also be who they are and be someone just like you, which may be a bisexual who is one of the following:

singer	athlete	detective
dancer	pastor	father
author	attorney	mechanic
construction worker	judge	aldermen

We need to let go of the bisexual and homosexual stereotypes so we can grow together and not separately.

CHAPTER 12

The Meaning Of DL And Gay Code Words

In the DL bisexual and gay culture, you may be confused. In some cases, they are and in other cases, they are not intended to be offensive or slanderous. In the DL, bisexual, and gay world, these word are used as codes. Or what are called identifiers. Identifiers are just that—words to identify oneself.

bottom: Someone who strictly receives anal penetration. This person's mannerisms and physical build can be either feminine or masculine.

boy: The one who looks and appears like a straight guy but is not straight at all. This is the guy the DL man can be seen with in public or with the family.

bitch: The one who may have feminine characteristics and plays the role of the female.

clock or clocked: When a male looks at another man and knows for a fact or strongly believes that the other man has sex with other men.

daddy: The man who looks like a straight masculine man and no one can tell or suspect that he has sex with other men.

diva: A homosexual fem male who flaunts his femininity freely in public as well as in private. He fits the gay stereotype.

fag/punk: A passive or aggressive homosexual whose sexuality maybe feminine.

family/friend/partner: A secret male lover or sex partner, someone who shares the lifestyle or is accepting of another's sexuality.

fuck around/mess around: Have sex with other males.

fully versatile: Must give as well as receive penetration and/or oral.

straight: A man who has sex with other men but do not receive penetration but may or may not give oral sex.

snow: Someone who has sex with others outside of his race.

top: The male who penetrates but would never receive penetration.

trade: Straight-looking masculine men whom you would not suspect to have sex with gay men, but he does. He may have sex with other men in exchange for food, money, lodging, clothes.

versatile: A man who receives and gives penetration.

versatile bottom: The man whose primary sexual position is to receive penetration. His secondary sexual position is to do the penetrating.

versatile top: The man whose primary sexual position is to do the penetration. His secondary sexual position is to receive penetration.

queen: Gay male who fits the mainstream stereotype.

Bisexual fathers have asked me, "Do you think my son will grow up to be bisexual or gay?"

Heterosexual fathers of bisexual/homosexual males say

ABOUT THE AUTHOR

I was born and raised in the poorest neighborhood in Missouri and Illinois. We lived on welfare and Section 8. I am a survivor of childhood sexual abuse and was terrorized throughout school for being a homosexual. I dropped out of high school and just received my high school diploma in 2007. I write at a seventh- to eighth-grade level. So if you notice errors in this book, hang in there with me. This ghetto-raised young adult will tell you how it should be told as it should be told.

I am an African American totally gay black male who has had sex with bisexual DL men. I have all the dirt on the down-low men who are married, single, dating, attached, or engaged to someone of the opposite sex. Remember that other DL books were written by well-educated black men with lavish lifestyles, who do not know anything about the rough urban street version of the down-low secret society and alliance. They cannot tell you about the poor, welfare, Section 8, working poor, down-low version. I am here to do just that!

DL men are really nervous and uneasy about this book's being released. They should be. DL men should know that they are human. Their sexuality is a birthright, but they should not deceive females about their lifestyle.

Many DL men feel that this book may disrupt their family and social life. I say to these men that you are not the victim, but your female partners are. My questions to you are as follows:

Do you believe or feel she has a right to know?

Are you neglecting or mistreating your male partner? Why?

Why are you deceiving her?

Why don't you get yourself a female who knows and accepts your alternative lifestyle?

I am the one to bring it to you raw and uncut. I am infamously known as Busta. The rumor was that I was dead. I have been approached many times by different people telling me that they heard I was dead. I had one guy tell me that he was at my funeral. The most current rumor is that I am serving time in the penitentiary. People have burned bread on me many times. For the record, I am alive. I have been living a sheltered life, living on social security, and fed up with these DL men with girlfriends and wives using and mistreating their male lovers and leaving them out to dry.

Several local African American male celebrities that I personally know who have mutual contact with one another have tested positive for HIV. They would have local DL parties for other DL men who made good money and are educated. One of those who have tested HIV-positive wants to come out and prosecute and accuse me, his secret male lover of ten years, of infecting him with HIV. I felt that out of all his other male sex partners, he had chosen to accuse me as a suspect because I was the most vulnerable, meaning that I had no money or do not know the right people to fight his allegations. He saw me as a weakling. He picked me out of all his more educated, independent male lovers.

While maintaining a fiancée, he wants to keep his name and celebrity status under wraps and do not want this information to go public. Too late! This portion of the book has been revisited as of June 2009 before any criminal charges or sentences get finalized. The other more popular, successful famous celebrities who have also tested positive for HIV refuse either to file any charges or to take on any actions toward anyone. They feel that they are responsible for their own actions and the outcome of their HIV-positive status as well. Their name, image, money, success, fame, and contracts are too important, and they will keep their anonymity. Well, I know who they are and will respect their request. We will remain cool and in contact. Well, let me tell you about the one who wants to file charges and see me locked up. Before I tell you the story, let me mention that this book may not get out in a timely manner. I hope that I reach the public at the time of the trial and before the sentencing/ruling of the judge and jury. I wish to be contacted by radio, magazine, papers, and television to tell my story candidly. So if any readers have any connections, you may contact me through my publishing company, Xlibris Corporation or through Xlibris.com.

I will not mention any names as of yet. But I will in book 2.

My previous male lover of ten years was a poor black kid from the urban city of St. Louis. Nowadays, he is a well-known celebrity in Missouri who lives a lavish lifestyle, engaged to marry his fiancée. (He has children from his previous female.) Before he had become famous, we both lived in poverty and struggled to make it day by day the best way we knew how. Once he began to gain popularity, he began to act shadier toward me. We continued our relationship, but I was to be kept his undercover secret. He abused me psychologically and physically throughout the ten-year relationship. I felt that I could not call the police on him during any abusive situation because I also wanted to protect his family and celebrity image. I always said to myself that no relationship was perfect, so for the sake of the relationship, I dealt with the abuse. I believed that once his children become grown enough to take care of themselves, both he and I would be together more openly. He had fallen for some female he had recently met and was spending more time with her than me. He felt that it was time to kick me to the curb after ten years. March 2009, he feared that I might show up to sabotage his relationship with his family and fiancée. He feared interference with his future wedding plans or that I would show up at his upcoming engagements. He said that I know too much personal information about him and that I was getting too involved and that I was getting too close with his family and celebrity lifestyle. We both knew that I knew more about him than she did. He knew that I had factual legal evidence that we were involved and there was no way this information must leak out to the public. So he created a criminal plot to quietly send me off to prison, which was supposed to make me disappear to prevent his family and fiancée from knowing that I ever existed. He also used this plot to get out of his contract and to gain popularity as a victim of HIV exposure, the same as Earvin "Magic" Johnson. (This criminal case is still under investigation as of June 2009.) The criminal case is recklessly infecting someone with HIV/AIDS. (I told him that I was positive before we had any type of sexual contact whatsoever and this was before he was famous.) Ten years later, this celebrity tests HIV-positive and claims that he did not know I was also positive. During this investigation, I had to put an order of protection out on him due to his harassments and threats. He scared the shit out of me to the point where I did not show up to the arraignment for the protection order. I had me in fear of his alliance and that they would also be there, recognize my face so that the next time one of his alliance members would see me, they could retaliate. Here's that story.

I first talked to Celebrity over the telephone dating, sex telephone line called Telepersonals. During our first conversation, I said, "There is something I have to tell you, I am HIV-positive." He paused a second then went on as if I had said nothing. We continued to talk, then out of the blue, he said, "What's your address?" He came right over that night. I lived in a building for seniors and those with disabilities. All guests have to sign in and show an ID and sign out when leaving. When he first came over, I was not under any type of control substance. I could not tell if he was or not.

I moved to a new apartment in October 1997. Celebrity and I continued to have safe sex. Back then, he would come over every once in a while and was always drunk and we talked on the phone every once in a while. We always used condoms during this relationship. He sometimes wanted to go without one, but I always made him wear one. We continued this relationship from 1995-1999.

I reconnected by Celebrity's leaving me a Yahoo! Instant Message from the Sex Personals. In the text, I gave him my address; he asked if he could bring his bag to change for work the next morning and I told him yes. This was Super Bowl Night of February 2007. He came right over that night. He had someone drop him off. He came in the door drunk, and I had already been drinking alcohol too. Although we were both drunk, we used condoms. He started catching the cabs or the bus to my house and leaving off to work the next morning. He would call me from his cell phone to ask if he could come over. He was coming over at least two to three. In the beginning of this relationship, I would say that we both are the type of people who like to listen to music while getting drunk and have sex while drunk. We often talked about life and family problems or his girlfriend and his baby's mother's problems. Sometimes he would get drunk and be verbally abusive, making threats, arguing, and making demands on me.

In 2008, he bought a car and two to three times a week would come by after dropping his kids off at school. He would usually arrive at 8:20 AM and leave at 8:40 AM. At other times, he would come in the evening and sometimes spend the night. During this time, his abuse became physical. He choked me to the point to where I was almost unconscious for touching him. I notified friends thereafter to make them aware of each visit. Yes, I did continue to have him over after the abuse. I felt that it was something I did that caused the attacks and abuse. So I continued to have him over, just try to be a good companion to my partner and not to upset him.

I have three witnesses verify my claims or his abuse because they were my safe callers in case something negative was to happen to me.

At no time during the relationship were we exclusive partners. We both had accounts at adult sites and met and saw other people.

In 2009, he became more controlling and abusive. He came over February 16 and started asking me questions about HIV. Later, he told me he had tested positive. He became highly upset that he would have to tell his girlfriend. He seemed terrified of having to tell his girlfriend about his gay lover. I asked if he had been with someone other than me and not used protection. He said it didn't matter, he had it, and he had to tell his girlfriend and his children's mother. He kept saying she would kill him if she knew he had sex with someone he knew was infected. He kept saying you have to help me with this. I didn't know what he meant, but I knew that look in his eyes. It was the look he had before he choked me. I was scared and said I'd help him. He said that from this point on I should talk as if I had just become infected.

As far as him passing the virus to his fiancée, I do not know but will not comment on her in this book. She is the real victim, but that's because of his secret lifestyle. I feel that I have been honest.

I decided to write this book very quickly before any criminal charges were carried out or finalized. I could not allow him and other men like him to continue to get away from the similar types of abuse and mistreatment of their male lovers. I felt that women needed to know. I decided to do this brief tell-all book about the down low from an urban, poverty, ghetto, and street perspective, which is not only putting females at a higher risk of contracting HIV/AIDS, but so much more. This book is not in any way to demonize bisexual men. It's to inform and educate, as well as uplift our men, and to let them know that it is fine to celebrate who they are. Just do not lie.

These bisexual men speak against homosexuality but will turn around and have homosexual sex in dark places. This is a very serious issue as well. It is also an action men who have sex with me taught me to do.

I am writing this guidebook with my back against the wall, meaning I am rushing to get this book published and out to the public before he succeeds in carrying out his threats or some form of preventing the release of this guidebook. (He does not know that this book is being written.) If he did know about this book, I am sure he has the resources and the money to stop the publishing of this book and can afford attorneys to fight any legal disputes against me and to halt any marketing, which will expose him. The problem he is facing with me right now is that he cannot go public due to his popularity and famous name. I am protected only because he cannot risk being public with this matter. If this does go public, my book will make millions off his name alone and he doesn't want that. He wants me to suffer. Oh my god, what if his fiancée find out that this book is about her man?

When this book gets published, he will be pissed. He will know I am talking about him, even she may get suspicious and say, "Damn, that sounds a bit like me." But I say to him, "I did not mention your name" and "Do not tell on yourself. Let it go. I will not bother you or call out your name. Your own personal actions will out you. What we had is over. I have gone on with my life, so you should go on with yours as well. Please do not come after me; neither you nor I need the drama." Well, the publicity and scandal will help my marketing and book sales and popularity. You do not want that, do you?

Let's go on with our lives living in a free world. There is no one to blame or fault. You did this to us. I was the perfect love. Now that you have been making it big over the years. Still, to this day, you are in the local papers, on television, and doing interviews. You're leaving me stuck in the dark with nothing to show for what we had. If anything negative were to happen to me, you will be their first suspect and this book will go on the New York Times *Best-sellers List.*

One,
Busta

www.ingramcontent.com/pod-product-compliance
Lightning Source LLC
Chambersburg PA
CBHW031329290526
45784CB00014B/2453